MARVELS and MYSTERIES

PIRATES

Paul Mason

Smart Apple Media

This edition first published in 2005 in the United States of America by Smart Apple Media.

Smart Apple Media
1980 Lookout Drive
North Mankato
Minnesota 56003

First published in 2005 by
MACMILLAN EDUCATION AUSTRALIA PTY LTY
627 Chapel Street, South Yarra, Australia 3141

Visit our website at www.macmillan.com.au

Associated companies and representatives throughout the world.

Library of Congress Cataloging-in-Publication Data

Mason, Paul, 1967-
    Pirates / by Paul Mason.
    p. cm. – (Marvels and mysteries)
    Includes index.

    ISBN 1-58340-772-3

    1. Pirates—Juvenile literature. I. Title.
    G525.M2258 2005
    910'4'5—dc22

                                                    2005042609

Edited by Vanessa Lanaway
Text and cover design by Karen Young
Page layout by Karen Young
Illustrations by Jacqui Grantford
Maps by Karen Young
Photo research by Jes Senbergs

Printed in China

Acknowledgments

The author and the publisher are grateful to the following for permission to reproduce copyright material:

Front cover photograph: Buccaneer ship, courtesy of Photodisc.

Texture used in cover and pages, courtesy of Photodisc.

Ancient Art & Architecture, p. 11; The Art Archive, pp. 22, 27; British Library, pp. 5, 13; Coo-ee Historical Picture Library, pp. 16, 26; Corbis, pp. 4, 7, 12, 29; Getty Images, p. 6; Mary Evans Picture Library, pp. 15, 25; National Maritime Museum, p. 18; Peter Newark's Historical Pictures, pp. 8, 9, 10, 14, 19, 20, 21, 24, 28; Photodisc, p. 17.

While every care has been taken to trace and acknowledge copyright, the publisher tenders their apologies for any accidental infringement where copyright has proved untraceable. Where the attempt has been unsuccessful, the publisher welcomes information that would redress the situation.

CONTENTS

GLOSSARY WORDS

When a word is printed in **bold**, you can look up its meaning in the glossary words box, and on page 31.

TIME

Some of the stories in this book talk about things that happened a long time ago, even more than 2,000 years ago. To understand this, people measure time in years Before the Common Era (BCE) and during the Common Era (CE). It looks like this on a timeline:

2000 1500 1000 500   0   500 1000 1500 2000 2500

Years BCE   Years CE

"PIRATES!"

For almost 4,000 years, one word has been guaranteed to strike fear into the hearts of sailors. In the Mediterranean, the Caribbean, and the South China Sea, the warning shout of "Pirates!" has meant death and destruction to honest seafarers.

During the 1800s, pirates were seen as monsters in human form. Pirates could be terribly cruel. One pirate captain used to cut off his victims' fingers if they were too slow handing over their rings.

····› Many pirates had their own flag.

What is a pirate?

Today we use the word "pirate" to describe many different kinds of fighting sailor. All pirates have three things in common:

1. They use violence to capture goods that do not belong to them.

2. They are sailors. Even when pirates attack on land, they always return to their ships to escape.

3. All pirates act illegally. If they are caught they will be punished—sometimes with death.

PEOPLE FILE

Bartholomew Roberts

Active as pirate: 1720–22

Description: Roberts was probably the most successful pirate ever. He captured over 400 vessels.

Famous for: Roberts wore fancy clothes and drank only tea. He died after being shot in the throat during a battle with the crew of an English warship.

Pirate captain William Kidd was so famous that thousands of people gathered to see him hanged in 1701. The rope broke and Kidd fell into the mud below. He was killed on the second try.

Early PIRATES

Location: Mediterranean and Black Seas
Date: from 2000 BCE onward

The first Mediterranean pirates were disorganized. They acted alone or in small groups, seizing whatever **plunder** they could locate. Later, though (from about 150 BCE), pirates became more organized. They became a terrible threat to shipping. In the end, the pirates clashed with the might of the **Roman Empire**.

Who were the first pirates?

The first pirates were Phoenician sailors from the eastern Mediterranean. They traded across the sea from about 2000 BCE. Many Phoenicians were honest traders, but others were pirates. They attacked ships and towns near the coast. The Phoenicians also kidnapped people and sold them off as slaves.

Walking the plank probably never happened, except in movies. Pirates were more likely to just throw people overboard.

Cilicians and Caesar

From about 150 BCE, pirates from Cilicia (now part of Turkey) began to terrorize the eastern Mediterranean. In 75 BCE they kidnapped a wealthy young Roman named Julius Caesar (Caesar later became Emperor of the whole Roman Empire). A **ransom** was paid and Caesar was set free. He promised the pirates he would have revenge. They laughed at his threats but Caesar hunted them down. He cut the pirates' throats and had them nailed to trees.

PEOPLE FILE

Pompey the Great

Lived: 106–48 BCE

Description: One of the Roman Empire's greatest generals.

Famous for: Pompey freed the seas of Cilician pirates. He attacked their bases and offered them land if they would give up piracy. Most surrendered.

Died: Killed in Egypt, after a long rivalry with Julius Caesar.

····> A great general, Pompey was known as "Magnus"—Latin for "Great One." His armies conquered parts of Asia Minor, Syria, and Palestine for the Roman Empire.

GLOSSARY WORDS

plunder	the profits of a robbery
Roman Empire	in power from about 275 BCE to 476 CE, the Roman Empire controlled much of Europe, and parts of Asia and Africa
ransom	a price demanded by kidnappers to set someone free

BARBARY Corsairs

The Barbary Corsairs came from the Barbary States on the North African Coast. These states were based around the cities of Algiers, Tunis, and Tripoli. The corsairs used fast, oar-driven **galleys** to attack **Christian** ships.

The corsairs were **Muslims** who operated with the approval of the ruler, or "*Dey*," of their home city. They thought of themselves as privateers. Their victims saw them as pirates.

What happened to corsair prisoners?

The corsairs used slaves to row the galleys they traveled in. Lots of the slaves were Christian seamen who had been captured by the corsairs. Many slaves were chained to their oars until they died.

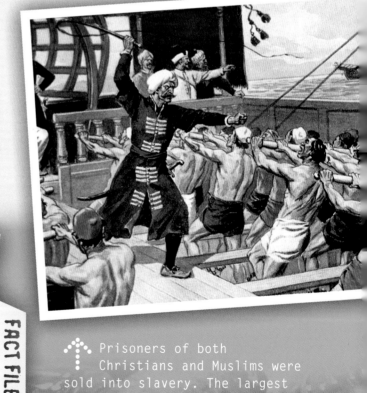

The *bagnio*

Some corsair prisoners ended up in the *bagnio*. This was a terrible prison:

• The slaves had to wear chains.

• Punishments included hangings and **impalement**.

Only a few ever escaped. Most who left were slaves whose families could pay a ransom to get them out.

FACT FILE

Prisoners of both Christians and Muslims were sold into slavery. The largest slave market in Europe was on the Christian island of Malta. Other prisoners ended up in the galleys, where few lived long.

Corsairs used galleys to attack enemy ships before boarding and fighting the enemy.

How did the corsairs attack?

The corsairs used a battering ram at the front of the boat to ram victims. Then they fired a cannon to clear the deck of the ship before boarding. When the deck was clear, the fighting men, or *janissaries*, poured onto the enemy ship. They were armed with muskets and **scimitars**.

FACT FILE

The corsair galley

Length: 180 feet (55 m)

Width: 16 feet (4.5 m)

Power: When fighting, the galley was powered by two rows of 16 foot (4.5 m) oars, each oar rowed by up to six men. When not fighting, a single mast and sail might be used.

Armaments: Usually one cannon in the **bow.** Up to 150 *janissaries* (soldiers).

GLOSSARY WORDS

galleys	large rowing and sailing boats
Christian	a follower of the Christian religion
Muslims	followers of the Muslim religion
impalement	being pierced through the body with a pointed object
scimitars	short, curved swords
bow	the front part of a boat or ship

Who were the most feared corsairs?

The most feared corsair captains ever were two brothers named Aruj and Khair-ed-din Barbarossa. During the early 1500s the Barbarossas built up a powerful **fleet** of corsair galleys. The brothers became the terror of the Mediterranean, attacking every enemy ship they saw.

One of Aruj's greatest successes came in 1504. He captured two treasure ships belonging to the Pope. The Pope was the head of the Christian religion. The whole Christian world was enraged.

HORUSCE en HAREADEN BARBAROSSA

Simon Danziker

Active as corsair: early 1600s

Description: A Dutchman who "turned Turk," becoming a Muslim corsair.

Famous for: Capturing over 40 ships in just two years.

Died: In 1611, hanged after being captured by Christian forces.

PEOPLE FILE

The greatest-ever corsair captains, Aruj and Khair-ed-din Barbarossa. The brothers originally came from Greece, but arrived in North Africa in the early 1500s.

The death of Aruj

In 1516 Aruj seized control of Algiers. The Spanish government decided his attacks on shipping had to be stopped. They sent 10,000 men to rid the seas of the Barbarossas. The corsairs fled, carrying their treasures with them. Weighed down by their gold, the corsairs were easily caught as they crossed a river. Aruj and most of his men died.

Khair-ed-din

Khair-ed-din escaped from Algiers. He became an ally of the Turkish Sultan. The Sultan was the most powerful ruler in the Muslim world. Khair-ed-din ended up as **Admiral** of the Sultan's fleet. People say that he lived to a fine old age, surrounded by luxury.

Dragut Rais, one of the cruellest of all corsairs. Dragut defeated a Spanish fleet near Jerba in North Africa in 1560. He was killed at the Siege of Malta in 1565.

PEOPLE FILE

Dragut Rais

Active as corsair: 1547–1565

Description: Khair-ed-din's fiercest **lieutenant**.

Famous for: Dragut once became so angry with one of his sailors that he had him burnt alive. It was punishment for the "crime" of breaking a grapevine while picking some grapes.

GLOSSARY WORDS

fleet	a group of warships, commanded by an Admiral
Admiral	leader of a group of ships
lieutenant	a person who does the wishes of someone else

The Privateers

Location: the Spanish Main and elsewhere
Date: 1400s and 1500s

Privateers were pirates who fought their country's enemies with government permission. For example, the governments of France and England allowed their ships to attack Spain's. The privateers had to give most of their booty to the government. Even so, they could become fabulously rich.

Sir Francis Drake is one of England's greatest heroes. Stories say that his drum, which hangs in the hallway of his old home in Devon, England, sounds whenever England is threatened by enemies.

Who was the greatest privateer?

Elizabeth I was Queen of England from 1558 to 1603. Under her command England became a great sea power. The greatest of Elizabeth's captains (who she called "sea dogs") was Sir Francis Drake. The Queen called Drake "my dear pirate." It was no wonder. One of his expeditions against England's Spanish enemies earned her $566,690 (£300,000). In those days this was a huge fortune.

12

Drake the navigator

Drake was a great navigator. He was only the second person ever to sail around the world, in his ship the *Golden Hind*. He had not planned to sail round the world. He kept heading west to escape his Spanish enemies, and ended up crossing the Pacific and Indian Oceans!

François le Clerk was a French privateer. He was famous for his daring attacks on harbors and coastal towns. He had a wooden leg, and was known as Pegleg.

Drake attacks!

Sir Francis Drake was a fearless privateer who made many attacks on England's Spanish enemies:

- **1572:** Drake captures Spanish ships and loots Nombre de Dios in Panama.

- **1577–80:** As part of his voyage around the world, Drake captures various Spanish ships. Among them is the treasure ship *Cacafuego*.

- **1585:** Raids on Spanish territories in the Caribbean. Drake holds the town of Cartagena to ransom.

- **1588:** Drake's greatest moment, as he fights a Spanish attempt to invade England. Spain's "invincible **Armada**" is sunk, and the Spanish invasion is stopped.

GLOSSARY WORDS

Armada   a large fleet of warships

Buccaneers

The buccaneers were pirates who haunted the Caribbean Sea from the 1630s onwards. They include Henry Morgan, Blackbeard, and William Dampier, some of the most famous pirates of all.

The first buccaneers lived on the Caribbean island of Hispaniola. They were settlers, runaway slaves, and escaped criminals. The thousands of pigs that ran wild on the island provided the people with food. They cooked the pigs on barbecues called *boucans* or *buccans*. This was how the buccaneers got their name.

PEOPLE FILE

Sir Henry Morgan

Active: 1660s and 1670s

Description: The greatest buccaneer of all, Morgan was a Welshman who ended up as Deputy Governor of Jamaica.

Famous for: Morgan conquered Panama, the wealthiest city in the **New World**, in 1671.

The buccaneers made their home on the island of Hispaniola.

14

When did the buccaneers become pirates?

The buccaneers became pirates when the Spanish invaded Hispaniola and killed all the pigs. They did this because the buccaneers had been selling pigs to passing privateer ships, which were enemies of Spain. The buccaneers had to move to the nearby island of Tortuga. They turned to piracy as a way of making a living.

PEOPLE FILE

William Dampier

Active as pirate/sailor: 1679–1711

Description: Dampier joined the buccaneers in 1680, and was a pirate and privateer for years.

Famous for: Dampier was a brilliant navigator who circled the world three times. In 1699 he commanded HMS *Roebuck* on a voyage of discovery to "New Holland"—now better known as Australia.

> William Dampier was an unusual buccaneer, because he was also a scientist and natural historian. Dampier also wrote several books, including *Voyage to New Holland in the year 1699*. "New Holland" was an early name for Australia.

GLOSSARY WORDS

New World   an old name for the Americas

The buccaneer way of life

The buccaneers decided to try a new way of life, one that was fair to all. Before a raid they would meet to discuss their plan. Their overall leader was called The Admiral of the Black. He listened to anyone who wanted to speak before making decisions.

Who were the Brethren of the Coast?

The buccaneers began to call themselves the **Brethren** of the Coast. Unlike other ships at the time, they tried to be **democratic**. A buccaneer ship's crew elected their own captain, and they could fire him too. The captain had to work alongside a group called the **Fo'c'sle Council**, who represented the crew in any discussion.

FACT FILE

The round robin

- Buccaneer ships recorded the crew's names in a "round robin." This was a list of the crew, written in a circle.

- The "round robin" meant that no one's name was at the top of the list. They could not be singled out for special punishment if the list fell into the wrong hands.

Strict rules determined which share of the loot each crewman got. Usually the pirates only divided their gains after they had collected a certain amount of money.

How was the loot shared out?

Buccaneers divided up their loot according to strict rules. The captain got the biggest share, while the most junior member of the crew got the least. Everyone knew before an attack what their share would be.

Cruel captains

Some buccaneer captains were famous for their cruelty. Roche Brasiliano, a Dutchman, roasted several Spaniards alive because they would not show him where they kept their pigs. Montbars of Languedoc, a French buccaneer, would pull out the guts of prisoners through a hole in their stomach.

Many buccaneers started small and worked their way up to a bigger ship.

Spared the noose!

- Piracy was a serious crime, punishable by death.

- Any pirate who was caught risked being hanged, though this was more likely for senior crew members.

- The only members of a pirate crew who were sure to escape were the surgeon and the musician. They had such rare skills that they would be put to work for whoever captured them.

GLOSSARY WORDS

brethren	brotherhood
democratic	giving everyone the chance to share in decisions
Fo'c'sle Council	a group of buccaneers who represented the crew in discussions and decision-making

The last days of buccaneering

By about 1660 many buccaneers had moved from Tortuga to Jamaica. They continued to attack Spanish treasure ships and became even stronger. No one would have guessed that the end of buccaneering was just a few **decades** away.

The British authorities had welcomed the buccaneers to Jamaica. They thought that the Spanish would not dare to attack with so many pirates around! Some pirates even became privateers. The Governor gave them permission to attack Spanish ships on behalf of the English government.

Port Royal

The buccaneers made their base in Port Royal, Jamaica. Port Royal was filled with pirates and other criminals. In 1692 the city was destroyed in an earthquake. The buccaneers had lost their home.

The Port Royal earthquake killed 2,000 people almost immediately. Two thousand more died of disease or injury soon afterward.

By the time this happened, many buccaneers were already leaving the Caribbean. Spain was sending less treasure home from the Americas, so the Spanish treasure ships were becoming rare. The buccaneers began to chase richer **prizes** in the Indian Ocean.

The Pirate Code of Conduct

Pirates often had to swear to follow the Pirate Code of Conduct. The Code set strict rules that pirates had to follow, such as:

- Men who stole from the ship's treasure had their noses slit and were **marooned**.

- Anyone trying to leave the ship was marooned with some gunpowder, a small gun, and a flask of water.

- Anyone **deserting** during a battle would be executed.

- No one could leave until the ship had $1,890 (£1,000) worth of booty.

- Lights were to be turned out by eight in the evening. Anyone wishing to carry on drinking had to do so by moonlight, on deck.

- Musicians were allowed Sundays off.

- Anyone trying to smuggle women aboard would be executed.

The pirates punished wrongdoers harshly, by marooning them on a deserted island. This meant almost certain death. For loyal pirates there were benefits, including a kind of health insurance. Anyone who lost his right hand in battle, for example, was paid 600 silver coins.

GLOSSARY WORDS

decades	periods of ten years
prizes	ships captured in battle
marooned	left alone on an uninhabited island
deserting	running away, especially from a battle or conflict

19

PIRATES
of the
Indian Ocean

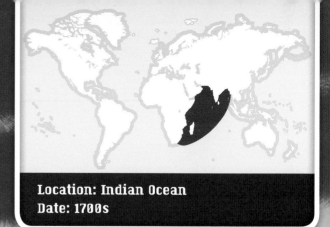

Location: Indian Ocean
Date: 1700s

Buccaneering began to die out in the Caribbean in the late 1600s. The Spanish treasure ships had become rare. Pirates began to look elsewhere for prizes, and they turned their attention to the Indian Ocean.

In 1695 Captain Henry Avery and his group of pirates attacked two Muslim ships on their way to India. The larger ship carried 800 men, but they put up little resistance. The captain of the Muslim ship told his crew to fight hard against Avery's men, then went and hid in his cabin!

PEOPLE FILE

Henry Avery

Active as pirate: 1690s

Description: One of the most famous pirates of his day, Avery was never caught.

Famous for: Avery was known for being vicious. During the attack on the *Gang-i-Sawai*, passengers were tortured and women jumped overboard to avoid facing his crew.

Died: No one knows for sure, but Avery is rumored to have died in about 1728.

◄···· Henry Avery took one of the richest prizes ever captured by a pirate. He was never caught, and no one knows for sure what became of him. Most historians, though, think Avery died in Devon, England in about 1728. Stories say that he had been swindled out of his fortune by merchants.

The Gang-i-Sawai

The large ship turned out to be the *Gang-i-Sawai*. It belonged to the Emperor of India. The cargo of treasure the *Gang-i-Sawai* was carrying was worth $615,000 (£325,000)—a vast fortune. The pirates stole all of it.

The Emperor of India was furious. In **retaliation** he stopped all trade with Britain. Next he threw all the British traders he could find in prison. The Emperor was determined to stop the pirate attacks.

Captain Avery chasing the *Gang-i-Sawai*. Pirate attacks on Moghul ships finally drove the Moghul emperor Aurangzeb wild with rage.

GLOSSARY WORDS

retaliation   paying back a wrongful act

Attacking the pirates

The Emperor of India stopped trade with Britain after the *Gang-i-Sawai* was attacked. A group of merchants in New York came up with a plan to prevent this happening again. They would hire someone to catch Avery and stop the pirate attacks.

The merchants chose Captain Kidd to pursue Avery. Kidd was a **retired** privateer. At first he wasn't interested in going back to sea. Then the merchants promised him a share of any captured pirate treasure. Kidd agreed to set sail.

Captain Kidd set sail from New York in the spring of 1696. His pirate-hunting expedition did not turn out quite as everyone expected.

William Kidd

Active as pirate: 1697–1699

Died: 1701

Description: Kidd was a Scottish former privateer who became a pirate-hunter, then a pirate.

Famous for: Kidd buried his treasure in various places along the East Coast of North America. He was arrested and hanged, and nobody ever found his treasure.

Captain Kidd set sail in 1696 aboard this ship, the *Adventure Galley*. He was supposed to be hunting pirates when he attacked the *Quedah Merchant*. The treasure of $18,890 (£10,000) was a huge fortune in those days.

The Quedah Merchant

Kidd set off in 1696 with a list of wanted pirates to catch. But he sailed straight past the pirates' base in Madagascar! Then, instead of hunting pirates, he became one. Kidd attacked two merchant ships. One, the *Quedah Merchant*, was full of treasure. Kidd and his crew made off with $18,890 (£10,000).

GLOSSARY WORDS

retired   no longer working at a particular job

The end of Captain Kidd

Captain Kidd returned home from the Indian Ocean in 1699. He found a hot welcome waiting for him in New York. The British government had issued a **warrant** for Kidd's arrest on charges of piracy.

Kidd was arrested and sent to England. He pleaded that his crew had forced him to raid other ships. Kidd also said that the *Quedah Merchant* had been flying a French flag. He said he had attacked it because at the time England was at war with France.

Kidd was found guilty of piracy and hanged in 1701. His death provided a cover-up for the wealthy New York merchants who had promised him a share of the pirate treasure. They were so eager to see him hanged that they even held back some evidence that might have cleared him.

Was Kidd telling the truth?

No one believed Kidd's story. He was hanged in 1701, and his body was put in a **gibbet** at Tilbury Fort. It served as a gruesome warning of what could happen to pirates!

In a final twist, several years later some old papers were discovered. They suggested that the *Quedah Merchant* had been flying a French flag. Had Kidd been telling the truth after all?

FACT FILE

What happened to Kidd's treasure?

- Several of Kidd's crew swore that he had buried treasure on Gardiner's Island, near New York City.

- Others said gold and jewels were buried elsewhere.

- No treasure was ever found—and to this day people are still searching for it!

> Legend says that the ghost of a dead pirate stands guard over the site where Captain Kidd buried his treasure. This hasn't stopped thousands of people trying to locate the huge fortune Kidd is said to have left behind.

GLOSSARY WORDS

warrant a written order

gibbet an upright post with an arm at the top, from which the bodies of criminals were hung

Notorious PIRATES

Location: Eastern seaboard of America and the South China Sea
Date: 1700s and 1800s

Throughout the history of pirates, a few names stand out. Some pirates stole fantastic sums of money. Other pirates were famous for being **eccentric**—like Bartholomew Roberts, who drank only tea. The really famous pirates, though, are the ones whose names struck fear in the hearts of all who heard them.

Ching Shih

The female pirate admiral Ching Shih was the terror of the China Seas in the nineteenth century. Ching Shih's husband had been a pirate leader. When he was killed, she took over command of his fleet.

FACT FILE

Pirate weapons of Southeast Asia

Pirates in Southeast Asia used a number of unusual weapons:

- *sumpitans*, or blowpipes
- spears
- the *dao*, a short scimitar-like sword.

Chinese pirates sailed in ships called junks. These were usually trading ships the pirates had captured. Larger junks had three masts and were about 80 feet (25 m) long.

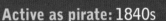 Chinese pirates attacking a European ship. The British Navy fought to destroy the Chinese pirates. They wanted to protect Britain's trade with China. The most famous battle happened in the Gulf of Tonking, when the pirate fleet of Shap-'ng-Tsai was destroyed.

PEOPLE FILE

Shap-'ng-Tsai

Active as pirate: 1840s

Description: Shap was the last great Chinese pirate admiral. He attacked ships and settlements south of Canton.

Career end: The British Navy destroyed Shap's fleet in 1849 and 1,800 pirates died. Shap escaped and lived to a ripe old age.

Resistance is useless

In 1806 a British officer reported on the terrible fate of those who resisted Ching Shih's pirates. The pirates had nailed an enemy's feet to the deck and then beaten him senseless. Finally, they rowed him ashore and cut him to pieces.

Ching Shih's fleet brought trade almost to a stop. Then a bitter argument between two of her captains began to divide the pirates. In 1810 they surrendered their ships to the Chinese government. In return, many were **pardoned**.

MINI FACT

Discipline was strict among the pirates. Anyone going ashore without permission had their eardrums burst. A second offense meant death.

GLOSSARY WORDS

eccentric   behaving unusually

pardoned   forgiven without punishment

27

Blackbeard!

Who was the most villainous pirate of all? In battle, black smoke poured from his hair. He was famous throughout the world for his ferociousness and cruelty. His real name was Edward Teach—but we know him as Blackbeard.

As a pirate captain from 1716–18, Blackbeard made a terrifying figure. His huge black beard was plaited and tied with ribbons. Before an attack, Blackbeard tucked fuses under his hat. These spewed out clouds of black smoke—his enemies must have thought they were battling some sort of demon!

Blackbeard's **flagship** was a 40-gun ship he had captured from the French. He renamed it the *Queen Anne's Revenge*.

FACT FILE

Blackbeard's pirate actions

Some of the things Blackbeard did as a pirate included:

- chopping off the fingers of victims to get at their rings
- holding the town of Charleston, South Carolina to ransom
- shooting his own men to keep them in line.

Cruel captain

Blackbeard was a cruel captain. Once, he was drinking in his cabin with his first mate, Israel Hands, when Blackbeard suddenly took out his pistols and shot the first mate in the legs. Hands walked with a limp for the rest of his days. Blackbeard said he did it because "If he did not now and then kill one of them, [his crew] would forget who he was."

◦◦◦◦◦ Blackbeard was a fierce fighter. As Maynard boarded his ship, Blackbeard shouted "Damnation seize my soul if I give you **quarter** or take any from you!"

MINI FACT

Blackbeard's pirate flag showed a skeleton holding a dart piercing a heart, and three drops of blood. In the other hand the skeleton held an hourglass.

FACT FILE

Blackbeard's death

Blackbeard was hunted down in 1718 by Lieutenant Maynard of the Royal Navy. Blackbeard died with 20 cutlass wounds and five pistol shots after battling with Maynard on the deck of his ship.

GLOSSARY WORDS

flagship   the ship that carries the leader of a naval force

quarter   mercy or forgiveness

A ROGUES' gallery

Chui Apoo

DIED

Description: Lieutenant of the Chinese pirate Shap-'ng-Tsai, later became a pirate leader in his own right.

Famous for: Apoo was a notorious pirate admiral based at Bias Bay, famous as a pirate haunt until the 1930s. Captured and tried after his fleet was destroyed in 1849, he committed suicide in prison.

Died: 1851

Jan Jansz
(also known as Murad Rais)

FATE NOT KNOWN

Active as corsair: 1620s

Description: Dutch privateer who became a Muslim corsair.

Famous for: Leading the most incredible corsair raid ever. Jansz led a fleet of corsairs to Iceland, raiding the town of Reykjavik and carrying off over 400 people as slaves.

Edward England

DIED

Active as pirate: 1718–20

Description: Pirate captain who was marooned by his crew for being too kind to prisoners.

Famous for: Escaping from his desert island by building himself a small boat, then sailing it to Madagascar. Bits of Edward England's story may have inspired the character Jack Sparrow in the 2003 film "Pirates of the Caribbean."

Died: circa 1720

Grace O'Malley

PARDONED

Active as pirate: 1560s–80s

Description: A female pirate leader based on Clare Island, on the west coast of Ireland.

Famous for: Giving up piracy in about 1586. O'Malley was later pardoned by Queen Elizabeth I of England.

"Calico Jack" Rackham

Active as pirate: 1718-20

Description: English pirate called "Calico Jack" because of his colorful cotton outfits.

Famous for: Having two women in his crew, one of whom, Anne Bonny, was his wife.

Died: 1720, hanged in Port Royal, Jamaica.

DIED

Anne Bonny

SURVIVED

Active as pirate: circa 1720

Description: A female pirate married to Captain "Calico Jack" Rackham.

Famous for: Defending her ship fiercely alongside Mary Read, another female pirate, while the rest of the crew hid in the hold. Escaped the death penalty by being pregnant at her trial.

GLOSSARY

Admiral leader of a group of ships

Armada a large fleet of warships

bows the front part of a boat or ship

brethren brotherhood

Christian a follower of the Christian religion

decades periods of ten years

democratic giving everyone the chance to share in decisions

deserting running away, especially from a battle or conflict

eccentric behaving unusually

flagship the ship that carries the leader of a naval force

fleet a group of warships, commanded by an admiral

Fo'c'sle Council a group of buccaneers who represent the crew in discussions and decision-making

galleys large rowing and sailing boats

gibbet an upright post with an arm at the top, from which the bodies of criminals were hung

impalement being pierced through with the body with a pointed object

lieutenant A person who does the wishes of someone else.

marooned left alone on an uninhabited island

Muslim followers of the Muslim religion

New World another name for the Americas

pardoned forgiven without punishment

plunder the profits of a robbery

prizes ships captured in battle

quarter mercy or forgiveness

ransom a price demanded by kidnappers to set someone free

retaliation paying back a wrongful act

retired no longer working at a particular job

Roman Empire in power from about 275 BCE to 476 CE, the Roman Empire controlled much of Europe, and parts of Asia and Africa

scimitars short, curved swords

warrant a written order

INDEX